## AND HIS MOUNTAIN
# The SUPERSTITION

### AND HIS MOUNTAIN
# The SUPERSTITION

THE UNIVERSITY OF ARIZONA PRESS
TUCSON          ARIZONA

THE UNIVERSITY OF ARIZONA PRESS

Copyright © 1972
De Grazia Gallery in the Sun
All Rights Reserved
Manufactured in the U.S.A.

ISBN 0-8165-0470-9
L.C. No. 72-192227

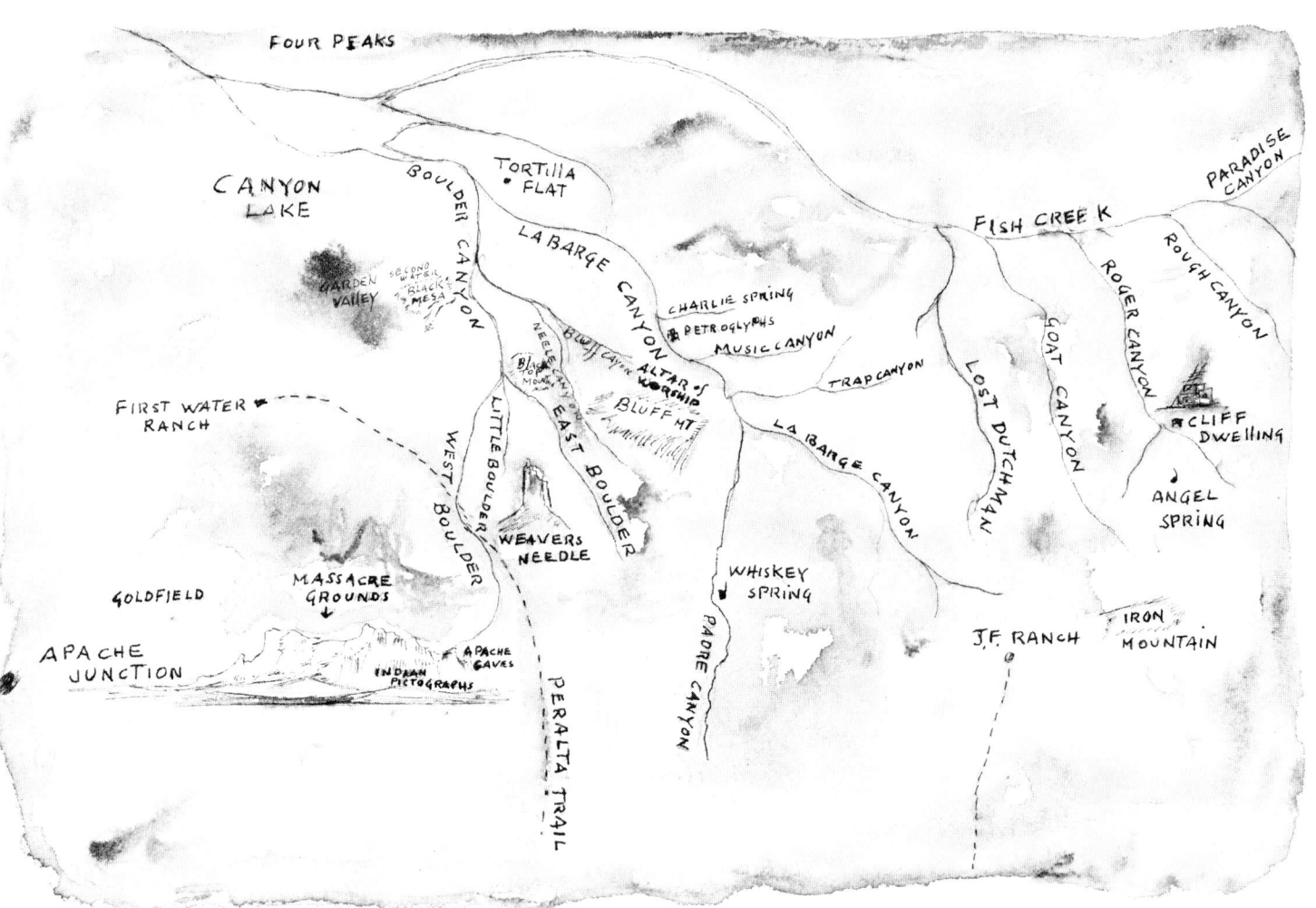

# CONTENTS

| | |
|---|---|
| The Superstition Mountain | 1 |
| Legends | 2 |
| The Prospector | 3 |
| Dangers and Delights | 4 |
| The Cliff Dwellers | 6 |
| Pictographs | 10 |
| The Stone People | 12 |
| The Little People | 14 |
| Padre Eusebio Francisco Kino | 16 |
| The Peralta Grant | 18 |
| The Lost Jesuit Treasure | 20 |
| A Map Is Discovered | 22 |
| The Peralta Expedition | 24 |
| The Massacre | 28 |
| After the Massacre | 32 |
| Apache Leap | 34 |
| Doctor Thorne | 36 |
| The Sacred Cave | 40 |
| The Dutchman | 42 |
| The Two Dutchmen in Arispe | 46 |
| The Dutchmen and Peralta in the Superstitions | 48 |
| The Mortal Wounding of Weiser | 52 |
| The Dutchman Leaves the Mine | 54 |
| The Dutchman's Last Trip | 56 |
| The Big Earthquake | 58 |
| Death of the Dutchman | 60 |

# THE SUPERSTITION MOUNTAIN

To me, the Superstition Mountain is full of mystery and intrigue. She is the most beautiful mountain in the whole world. At times she looks old, very very old, craggy and tired, and very sad. Yet at other times she looks young and lovely.

Once you see her you can't help but wonder about her and admire her beauty. You too will fall in love with her. The more you see her, the more attractive and magnificent she will become Soon you will succumb to her, and she will possess you completely. Then she will own you, because your thoughts will always be with her and you will want to be close to her.

She has quite a personality. She is alive. Her mood is ever changing. You can be close to her and yet feel so very far away. She bathes in rainbow colors. Her desert shadows are long and purple; they look like long eyelashes. She is truly like a queen of long ago, very very rich. But she can also be a bitch.

When I think of the Superstition Mountain, I think of the long chain of mountains extending from where she stands at Apache Junction and east to Superior. That is a long way. The western end is spectacular. Sheer cliffs and canyons cut deep, almost to the desert floor.

It is around Weaver's Needle, the stark shaft of rock, that the Indian legend of the stone people began. And it is there that the thunder gods and all the demons live. To be sure, it is the most "popular post."

In the winter this mountain range is lonely. Once in awhile the Mountain dresses in white. She is divine, pure, and holy.

Most of the summer she is dressed in hot colors. Then you are drenched with sweat and put through a wringer. But in the evening it will be nice for awhile. You will feel embraced and cuddled — left alone to contemplate in peace. There is a moment of silence, as in prayer. You will feel that you are in a monastery surrounded by never-ending cathedral canyons. You will remember that the poet has paid homage, ballads have been sung, writers for years have been telling her legend, the artist has captured the many moods of these mountains.

As the night comes upon you, the heavens will be sprinkled with jewel-like stars, and she, with mother-like assurance, ever so gently, will waft you away into your dreams, far away.

*De Grazia*

# LEGENDS

The Superstition Mountain is not only rich in gold, she is also rich in legends. A true story becomes a legend when the facts have been obscured and lost. As time goes on, the legend becomes so legendary that the story-tellers become lost in a mist; the picture will be out of focus, but they will believe in the legend.

One look at the Superstition Mountain tells me that these legends are very real.

> She is a big beautiful mountain,
>   guarding her gold.
>
> It is the nature of man to hunt, to search;
>   his mind is made of dreams.
>
> So forever he searches and searches,
>   until the end of his dreams.

The Superstition Mountain is a perfect setting for legends, a perfect place to sit around a campfire, a good place for hiding, a good place to be lost, a good place to dream about gold.

> She likes dreams.
>
> She likes legends.
>
> She guards her gold.

# THE PROSPECTOR

The prospector is a rare individual. He prefers to live alone, far away from civilization, far away alone with nature. His needs are few. He can get by with very little — almost nothing.

The prospector has become a symbol — an old man with a beard, a white beard, alone with his trusted burro. He disappears over the horizon into the mountains, always to follow the rainbow, seeking the pot of gold.

Every day brings new hope. He thinks that Lady Luck, maybe this time, this day, will smile on him and present him with a ledge of gold — a bonanza!

He spends all his waking hours roaming the hills, looking for a place rich in pay dirt. When he finds a place that looks like that, he settles down for some serious digging — trying here and there. He digs and digs and digs, hoping to find the vein of gold. The prospector has left many a hole in the mountain as he disappears over the horizon.

The prospector was once a young man with a black beard. But the days have gone into weeks, weeks into months, months into years — into many many years. Now he is old and his body bent. He looks toward his mountain, and he still daydreams.

He is sad. There is no place for him on his mountain anymore. He longs for one more glimpse of gold — one glimpse of the mountain's richness. He is still a little man, with only a burro, who has pointed the way for others who are waiting and ready to grasp his gold.

He is alone again.

# DANGERS AND DELIGHTS

The Queen Mountain reigns supreme. As searchers for gold come and go, she watches. She sets many traps — rattlesnakes, javelinas, empty waterholes. Many men have come and gone. Many have been lost, never to return. Yet the seemingly never-ending search goes on and on.

To the hapless ones who do not know the mountains, who come unprepared and stumble into their ill fate, the Mountain does strange things. That is where the danger lies. The mind becomes distorted, everything loses its proportion, then anything can happen.

On one of my treks into the Mountain, while riding on a narrow trail, we came around a bend. There in front of us, a bunch of javelinas were rushing toward us. The horses exploded. How on that narrow trail we managed to survive I'll never know.

Then there are the haunting sounds at night. A gunshot that cracked the silence, deep in the canyon as we tried to sleep — almost impossible when the moon is high. The horses stomping back and forth. Then the rattlesnakes hissing, the horses were nervous, we were nervous — no sleep that night.

In spite of the hardships and frightening experiences, I will return again to this Mountain, for there I have found beauty, exhilarating visions of nature's creations.

Others before me must have experienced the same feeling. The names they have left behind tell me so. In this Mountain they have found the Prayer Room, Angel Springs, and the Sacred Caves. And there is the Madonna of the Mountain.

One little prospector left behind a peach tree and a rose bush. But none are able to contribute much to this Mountain.

# THE CLIFF DWELLERS

In the middle of the Superstition Mountain there is a beautiful rugged canyon with crystal-clear water. In the sheer canyon rock is a natural cave. In the cave are the ruins of many rooms, with square corners, built out of flat rocks and caliche-like mud, plastered inside by hand. Thumbprints are still visible.

It was here that once upon a time the cliff dwellers lived. They were primitive. The place was isolated, it was a stronghold, it provided protection and coziness. They must have been a maverick group, an outlaw group. They were not numerous enough to protect themselves, but they lived where they had protection.

Evidence can still be found of the cliff dwellers existence — utensils, sherds of pottery, and small corn cobs, very small. This group, for sure, were farmers.

They did weaving out of fiber. Perhaps they made sandals. They were seed eaters and root eaters. They also ate flowers and berries, and a rabbit or two if they could catch one.

These prehistoric Indians left so long ago that nobody knows much about them, where they came from or where they went. When the modern Indian of today — Pima, Apache, Maricopa — came, the cave dwellings were in ruins.

So up to this writing, the story of the Superstition cliff dwellers is one of the mysteries of the Mountain. And for another age it will remain a puzzle.

# PICTOGRAPHS

Pictographs are graphic art. They can be found only where there are rocks. Whether they tell a story, whether they record time, a war, or a hunt, whether they were made for religious intent or to pass the time of day as an aesthetic thing, that too will remain a mystery.

But they are lasting inscriptions. They have lasted, exposed to all kinds of weather, for many years, many centuries.

The designs are made by picking on the rock with a smaller sharp rock. The picking is done on the dark side of the rocks. The majority of designs are of animals, such as sheep. Some of them are of human form, with square or circular heads.

Perhaps the design tells how to get to a certain place, or what one may find at the place indicated.

Time and the elements have given these rocks a beautiful patina. The overall effect to me is soothing and pleasing. I can't help but be spellbound, and often spend much time admiring their rock talk.

In the past I have used pictograph drawings for textile designs. And they have been successful.

Picking on rocks has been going on since the beginning of time.

# THE STONE PEOPLE

There is a legend about a big flood in the Superstition Mountain. It is a legend about the beginning of time and the end of time. It is a perfect legend, because as you look at the mountain from the south near the western end, you can see a white foamy strip, a limestone formation high up, running east around the cliff, and it looks like a water mark.

The Maricopa Indian legend sounds like a story from the Bible, of many many years ago.

They say the Earth Doctor made people out of clay, but he forgot to give these earth people the spirit of kindness and love. So the people were mean. They made trouble between one another. They simply did not want to be good to each other.

One day the Earth Doctor told the dreamy moon and the yellow sun to go away and not come back for forty days. Then the Earth Doctor pulled the sky down, and it began to rain and rain and rain. It rained forever.

The flood came, and the earth people got scared and ran up the pinnacle in the Superstition Mountain. Because they were bad, they pushed and ran over each other, and the flood kept going higher and higher.

Little birds started to cry, but a dog talked to the little birds. "If you keep on crying you are going to add water to the flood." So the birds flew high into the sky, and with their beaks held onto the sky. But the water kept going higher and higher. The people froze and turned to stone.

To this day you can see the foam marks of the flood, and the people are forever stone — human monoliths.

# THE LITTLE PEOPLE

While I was camping in the Superstition Mountain one evening, a Papago told me that a small group of little people lived there, and that the little people know everything and see everybody that comes into the Mountain. He said they probably are guarding the gold.

The little people are so scant that you barely get a glance at them. They ride rabbits, and you know how fast rabbits run.

The impish little people are primarily gold miners. They live in the mines. You hear stories about them in mining camps. They gather gold nuggets and hoard them. They always have a guard on watch.

If you ever see a puff of blue smoke close to the ground, follow it. It will be the little people smoking. They love to smoke.

Or if you ever see the footprints of the little people, follow them to the gold mine. If you ever catch up to where they are camped and surprise them, they will give you gold nuggets as a reward.

# PADRE EUSEBIO FRANCISCO KINO

One of the greatest names to be etched in the state of Arizona is Padre Eusebio Francisco Kino. Padre Kino was a Jesuit. He was born in Italy in 1645. He died in 1711 in Sonora, Mexico, 125 miles south of Tucson.

Kino established many missions in northern Sonora and southern Arizona. This padre came on horseback in 1687 with a cross and many prayers. He blazed many trails.

He was a cowboy of God, the first to drive cattle into Arizona for the Indians. He proved California to be a peninsula and not an island.

But best of all he brought Christianity, and the Indians loved him. He came, he gave, and he asked nothing in return.

His territory extended on the east to the San Pedro River near Benson, west to the Colorado River in Yuma, south to Sonora, and north to the Salt River.

Around 1695, Kino visited the ruins of Casa Grande. As he must have seen the Superstition Mountain to the north, a short distance away, I strongly believe he was impelled to visit that beautiful Mountain.

# THE PERALTA GRANT

King Ferdinand the Sixth of Spain in 1748 awarded Don Miguel Peralta of Arispe, Sonora, Mexico, a land grant which included the Superstition Mountain. The reason for this grant is lost in time.

The size is not clear. The northern boundary of the grant went east from the Salt River near Phoenix, to Globe, including the Apache Reservation (San Carlos), then to Morenci, where I was born, and through part of New Mexico. The southern boundary included Casa Grande, parts of the Gila River, Safford east to New Mexico (Silver City).

The Peralta family was the first to own, explore, discover and work the gold mines in the Superstition Mountain. For over one hundred years the Peraltas owned the Superstition Mountain, yet they never moved in and established a permanent camp. Never were there women on the expeditions. It may have been fear of the Apaches or of the Superstition's Thunder Gods.

The Peralta expedition went in and gorged gold from the mountain and returned to Sonora, Mexico. Nobody will ever know how many expeditions were made into the Superstition Mountain by the Peraltas. Nor will anyone ever know how much gold was brought out, or how many mines were discovered and operated.

The Peralta grant is often known as a church grant. It is known as a church grant because it was left in trust of a church in Arispe for safekeeping. So from 1748 to about 1845, for a century of generations, it was as though a curtain had been dropped.

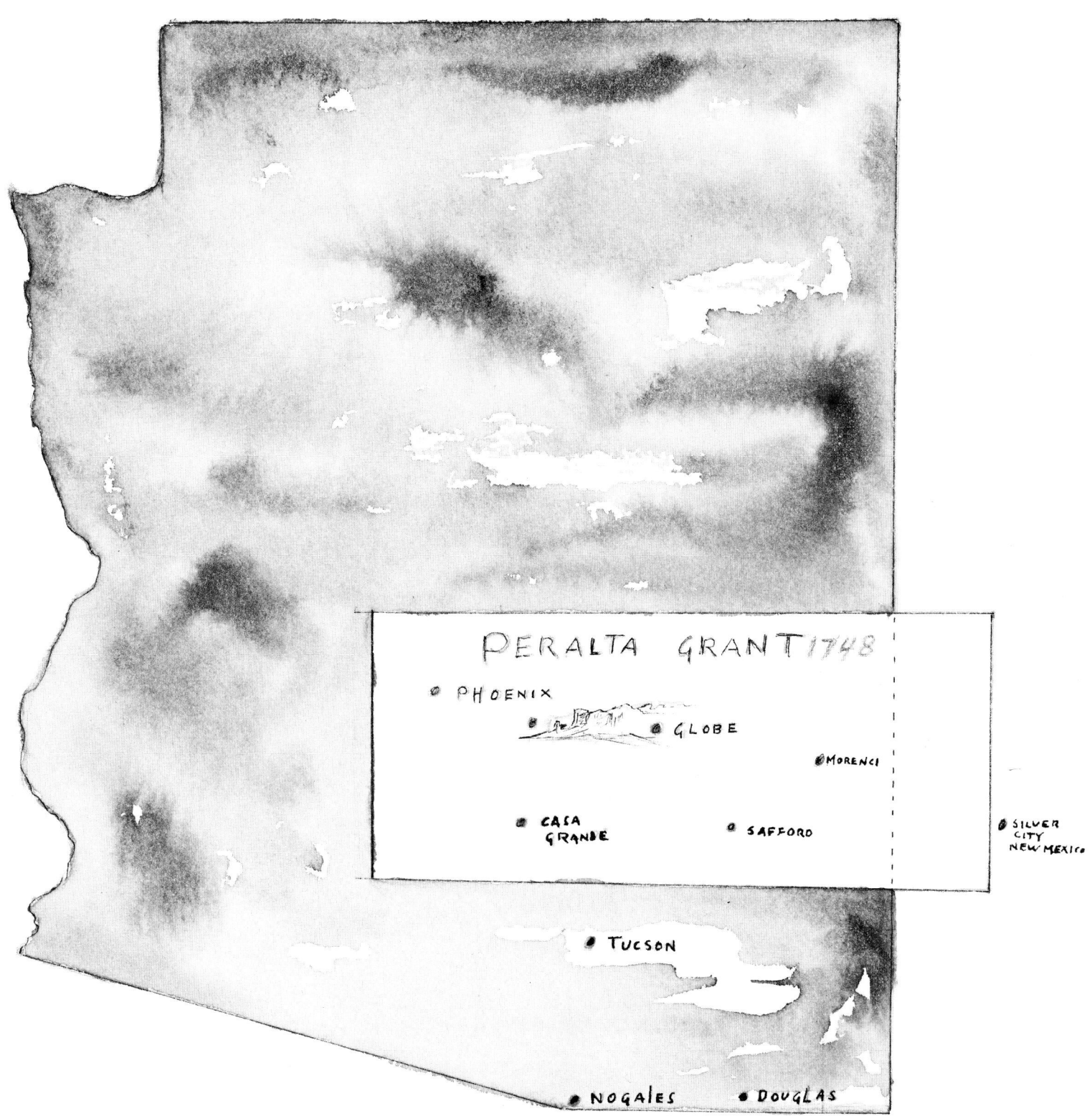

# THE LOST JESUIT TREASURE

One of the legends about the western slope of the Superstition Mountain is about Weaver's Needle. It is a legend of treasure. They say that Jesuit padres buried the treasure just before they were replaced by the Franciscans.

The story goes that the King of Spain, Charles III, was not receiving his share of one-fifth of the gold. It was said that some Jesuit padres had been keeping all of the loot.

In 1764 there was an expulsion, an exodus of the Jesuits. They were replaced by the Franciscans. The king was hoping for a better share of gold.

The Jesuits were aware of this forthcoming event, and they gathered from the missions and churches all of the religious valuables and treasures from southern Arizona and northern Mexico. Among the items were golden crosses, santos, chalices, and candelabras of pure gold and silver.

The Jesuits took these treasures to the Superstition Mountain and hid them around Weaver's Needle for safekeeping. The caravan was large, with many animals and heavy loads.

At some point along the mountains they were seen coming out. This time the caravans were empty.

# A MAP IS DISCOVERED

The golden spider web spins on and on. We know that directly and indirectly the legends of the Superstition Mountain were affected by Mexico, especially when Mexico broke the yoke from Spain in 1827.

A padre was sent to Arispe, home town of the Peraltas. As time went on the humble padre showed a great deal of interest in his priestly office. In the storehouse he rampaged through books and papers, official records. He went through trunks and boxes. He spent days looking for nothing in particular, but still looking for anything and everything. As he looked, he had great anticipation.

One day he came across the Peralta grant, a map on animal hide, about eight inches by twelve inches. Also he found sandstone carvings of the Peraltas' gold mine in the Superstition Mountain. With this treasure he was elated, but bewildered as to what he should do. After pondering for a few days and losing much sleep he wanted to get all the responsibility off his chest. He decided to pass the burden on to the Peraltas.

The padre talked to the Peraltas in hushed secrecy. The Peraltas were miners and ranchers, but they were not doing so well financially. Yes, they had heard stories of the grant to the north, rich in gold, but they had never seen it or known its exact location. This grant had happened almost one hundred years ago, and time had dimmed, distorted, and exaggerated facts, places, and names. But these people were descendents of the original Miguel Peralta, and they did show a great deal of interest — so much so that they organized an expedition to explore, locate, and work the Superstition for its gold.

# THE PERALTA EXPEDITION

The Peralta expedition was large and well organized, with many rifles for protection against the Apaches, and many peons to work the mines. The peons wore sandals, the soles made of cactus fiber.

The treasure-seekers brought with them many mules and horses, workmen, tools and supplies. They were strong and alert.

Day after day the expedition moved north to the unknown country. They wanted to move in, work the mine, uncover as much gold as possible and move out.

At night, guards were on watch in the Superstitions. Ramadas and rock corrals were established. The men slept in firebeds when the weather was cold and damp. They built an arrastra to crush the gold ore with mules.

They brought their own saint and built prayer rooms, places of worship. Who knows but what they even brought their own padres along.

Many times they went into the Superstitions and out. How much gold was taken out, no one knows. But they did go back again and again.

# THE MASSACRE

Many expeditions of the Peraltas went into the Superstition Mountain in 1848, and came out loaded with gold. The Peraltas were aware that the United States wanted to buy a big portion of land from Mexico — the Gadsden Purchase.

In the meantime the Apaches were intrigued, amused, and puzzled with all the activity in the Mountain. From a distance they eyed the noble mules as good eating.

Work was not the Apache way of life. Work was for the women. So the Apache bucks patiently waited, and waited, and planned an attack.

The Peraltas were alarmed as the Apaches increased in number. So they loaded the mules with gold ore for a quick exit. The Apaches would vanish, and reappear.

The heavily loaded mules moved slowly in the mountains. The Peraltas were worried, but there was no turning back. The whole atmosphere was tense. Gray clouds overhead cast sinister shadows. On each turn the expedition expected a sudden but brutal attack from nowhere.

Then, fast as lightning, the Apaches were on the poor Peraltas. The Peraltas were outnumbered, and it must have been sad.

# AFTER THE MASSACRE

Immediately after the massacre the Apaches prepared for a victory celebration.

Some of the mules with gold did run away. Others, wounded, stood trembling while the Indians cut the gold loose, scattering it over the ground.

Huge fires were built. The Indians killed the mules, cooked them, and ate them. The celebration went on for many days. I am sure the celebration lasted as long as the food lasted. They stayed until the last animal was eaten.

The squaws covered the Peralta mine so that no one could ever find it again. Much of the gold ore was hidden in caves and tunnels by the Apaches.

Day turned into night, and the Apaches silently vanished into the darkness, as though nothing had ever happened.

# APACHE LEAP

For a long time now the nomadic Apaches had been attacking and robbing the Pimas and Maricopas who lived in the immediate surroundings below in the flat land of the Superstitions.

The Pimas and Maricopas farmed the land. They were peace-loving Indians who lived in permanent homes built of mud and saguaro ribs.

From all of the marauding, the peaceful ones turned on the Apaches and surprised them — up the mountain they drove them.

Bewildered and confused and seeing no way out, the renegade Apaches leaped over the sheer cliff to their death.

To this day, the tears of the Apaches as they fell are found in abundance in the earth at the base of the sheer cliff. They are now beautiful little stones.

# DOCTOR THORNE

A military doctor at Fort McDowell, north of the Superstition Mountain, had cured various ailments of the Apaches. Now, in 1865, he was about to leave the fort.

The Apaches wanted to repay the kind doctor, so they decided to show him gold, knowing how the white man loved the yellow metal. They took him under one condition. He must go blindfolded.

They criss-crossed and zigzagged the canyons for many hours, up and down the mountains, until they finally got to the cave where the rich gold ore and nuggets were hidden. The gold and the tunnel were behind a waterfall.

They took off the blindfold and let the doctor see and take all the gold he could carry. He filled his saddlepack and his pockets.

Again they zigzagged back and forth. They crossed the river several times on their way back to the fort.

This doctor, named Thorne, years later made a few attempts to locate the cave, but he never found it again.

The secret belonged to the Apaches.

# THE SACRED CAVE

The Apache Thunder Gods live in the Superstition Mountain.

There are many caves in the Mountain, some are big, some are small. A cave is to protect something or someone.

One sees a cave and wonders about it.

Somewhere in the Superstition Mountain the Apaches have a sacred cave. Apache drums are heard at night. Bonfires light the side of the Mountain and chants are heard as the Indians dance in a circle.

One of the spectacular dances is the crown dance. The crown dancers' appearance adds much excitement to the religious rites.

What goes on is private. In the cave there is a secret. It could be gold. One wonders.

# THE DUTCHMAN

The most colorful and legendary figure of the Superstition Mountain was a German called Jacob Walz — the Dutchman. About 1871 he moved in and out of the Mountain, around the Mountain, about the Mountain, in a mysterious way. So all the legends with a spider-like web made of gold thread spin about him. He stands alone on the golden spider web on the Mountain. The legions of searchers for gold before and after him have been forgotten. The wonderful yet strange and sad tales of the romance of gold and the Dutchman have excited people from around the world.

I believe that the Dutchman was a man of great capacity, a man deeply sad and alone, a man who realized the responsibilities of the possession of gold, a man of great understanding. He knew where the gold was. Yet he left it where it was and tapped it only for his humble needs. He didn't gouge the heart of the Mountain and rob her of her gold. The gold is still there, somewhere. One day the Mountain again will lift her cloak of mystery and reveal more gold for those who appreciate its beauty.

A romantic note in the legend is that the Dutchman met a beautiful Apache maiden. At dusk one day the Dutchman and the maiden were seen headed toward the Mountain and at break of day they returned to the desert with a burro loaded with rich gold ore. Not long after their return, while the Dutchman was away, a band of Apache warriors appeared on horseback and carried the maiden with them, never to be seen or heard from again. She had revealed a sacred Apache trust. This brought sadness to the Dutchman. This was the price he paid for gold.

Another story is that Jacob Walz, the Dutchman, had a prospecting partner by the name of Jacob Weiser, another German, a friend of many years. They searched for gold together. On one of their trips to the Mountain, after prospecting all day they made camp near a spring in the evening. The Mountain was quiet. It was a still evening. Yet at a distance they could hear a hammer tapping on rocks, an unmistakable sound of mining.

With gun in hand, over the ridge, through the wash, over another ridge they went. To their surprise, two men without shirts were working a shallow tunnel. Indians working a gold mine? Impatience and greed made the Germans raise their guns and shoot. It was now dark, too dark. They returned to their camp. Early next morning they went back to investigate and found they had shot two Mexican miners. This could have been avoided, but it wasn't. So there was tragedy for the greed of gold.

# THE TWO DUTCHMEN IN ARISPE

The story of the Lost Dutchman Mine is filled with legends, legends which have many ramifications. Another tale of how the Dutchman — Walz — came to the Superstition Mountain as possessor of the Superstition mine is this one:

Walz and Weiser were prospecting in northern Mexico near Arispe. The town was celebrating the day for their saint — with music, food, and dancing.

One version of the tale is that the two Germans met Peralta in a cantina. They became friends, and they made a deal to go with Peralta into the Superstitions on an expedition for gold. After all, the Superstitions did belong to the Peraltas, through the grant.

Another version is that while the two Germans were in Arispe watching a gambling game, during a fiesta, Peralta was stabbed. The two Dutchmen rescued him, thus making them close friends, compadres. When Peralta got well, he invited them to join his mining expedition in the Superstition Mountain.

# THE DUTCHMEN AND PERALTA IN THE SUPERSTITIONS

How long the two Dutchmen and Peralta were on the Peralta mine is not known. They had gone there to work on the old grant. They must have had maps either on parchment or on stone like Moses' ten commandments.

By now the Superstition Mountain belonged to the United States, not to Mexico.

The men possibly rediscovered some of the rich mines, and perhaps discovered some new ones. In any event, the search was successful. Some rich gold ore was brought out.

The mules were loaded, and the expedition was on its way back to Mexico. Somewhere in the desert before they got to Mexico, Peralta made a deal with the Dutchmen. Peralta said, "Amigos Compadres, I think I keep all the gold, your share and mine, and you go back and keep my mine. It's all yours — but watch those devil Apaches."

The two Dutchmen accepted the offer and returned to the Mountain, while Peralta went back to Mexico.

# THE MORTAL WOUNDING OF WEISER

Things got worse now. In 1871 bad luck seemed to hit all around the Dutchman, like lightning. It hit every which way.

The Dutchman's partner, Weiser, was killed two times. Anyway, there are two different tales about it.

One version says that the Dutchman shot his partner so that he could have all the gold for himself. The other version is that while the Dutchman was away for grub — either at Pinal or Florence — the Apaches came to camp and shot arrows through Weiser and spread-eagled him and left him for dead.

Somehow Weiser, wounded, delirious with much pain, made his way to a Pima village. A friendly Pima Indian took him to Doctor Walker. The doctor eased the pain, and then Weiser died in the arms of the doctor — but not until he had given a map of the gold mine to the doctor.

The map to this day is nowhere to be found, but I am sure someone, somewhere, has it. Maybe it is at the bottom of somebody's trunk. Who knows. The map may lead to a ledge of gold.

The Dutchman never knew the fate of his partner, but the telltale destruction around the camp told him a lot. It was a tragedy.

# THE DUTCHMAN LEAVES THE MINE

The Dutchman covered his cache of gold ore and left the camp, planning never to return again. Gold, a metal so beautiful and pure, caused so much grief. He wanted no part of it, so he wandered from bar to bar, moved with the Maricopa Indians, to forget and be forgotten.

After much wandering he finally moved to Phoenix. Time was healing the wounds of tragedy. He acquired a piece of land in Phoenix and built an adobe room.

He raised chickens, perhaps to sell eggs. At least it was a quiet life. Age, too, was against him. He was over seventy years old.

While in Phoenix he became a friend of Mrs. Helen Thomas, owner of an ice cream parlor. She also baked bread. As time went on they became close friends. She was good to the Dutchman and sort of watched out for him.

The Dutchman, knowing of Mrs. Thomas' hardships, decided to make one last trip to the Superstition Mountain to bring back enough gold ore to help ease her way.

# THE DUTCHMAN'S LAST TRIP

The kindly old Dutchman headed for the Superstition Mountain, in 1878, for the last time, to uncover one of his caches of gold-rich pay dirt.

He emerged from the Mountain with a little gold ore for Mrs. Thomas.

I believe the Dutchman knew the value of gold, but he also knew that gold was a means to an end. Gold was not to be used in a vulgar way, for power, or to display wealth.

Gold had to be used in an humble way, with respect and only when needed.

# THE BIG EARTHQUAKE

To help upset the many legends, Mother Nature lent a hand about 1887. An earthquake rocked and tumbled, shaking up the Superstition Mountain.

Rocks and boulders were rearranged. The trail to gold mine shifted and vanished. Old landmarks disappeared. New canyons appeared with new springs and fresh waterholes.

When you gaze upon a Peralta map that will lead you to the lost Dutchman gold mine, remember the earthquake.

Who knows what lies beneath the boulders.

# DEATH OF THE DUTCHMAN

The year 1891 was a year of much rain in Arizona. Rain in the mountains made the rivers run high, strong, and wide. As the waters flowed to the flat lands of the desert, they spilled over and flooded — especially around the Phoenix area — from the Salt River in one direction and from the Gila River in the other direction.

The Dutchman, living alone, age eighty-one, must have been soaked and chilled. This made the poor old man weak. He never fully recovered. Finally he died and was buried in Phoenix.

He died in the Territory of Arizona, and with him forever will be sealed the true story of gold in the Superstition Mountain.

Men will come, hunt, and try to solve the beautiful, rich, colorful, golden legends of the Lost Dutchman Mine. They will never know for sure. When they die, other men will follow.

The legends will grow bigger and go on forever and ever. And as long as the Superstition Mountain is there, the legends will be there.

AMEN!

**WITHDRAWN**
No longer the property of the
Boston Public Library.
Sale of this material benefits the Library